Fishing for Snakes

and

Baking Apple Pies

Fishing for Snakes

and

Baking Apple Pies

Poems and Photography

Phil Lowe

Edited by Cathy Kodra

One Spirit Press
Portland, Oregon

©Copyrighted 2011 by Phil Lowe
Photography © 2011 Phil Lowe

All rights reserved
Printed in the USA

ISBN 978-1-893075-70-2
LCCN: 2011927061

Book Design: Spirit Press, LLC

This book may not be reproduced by electronic or any other means which exist now or may yet be developed, without permission of Spirit Press, except in the case of brief quotations embodied in critical articles and reviews.

One Spirit Press
www.onespiritpress.com
Portland, Oregon

Contents

Part I: Apple Seeds

Original Sin.....2
Mystery Woman.....3
Population Explosion.....4
Floating the Boat.....5
Breeding Division.....6
Bondage for Bread.....7
Rods-Snakes-Lice-Frogs.....8
Desert Storm.....10
Promised Land.....11
Roman Style.....12
Bible Age.....13
School Days.....14

Part II: Talking to the Creator

Higher Ground....18
Creepy Shadow.....19
Karma-Drama.....20
Light and Sound.....21
Time Line....22
Looking for Light....23
Above the Clouds....24
Music Within.....25
Echoes and Reflections.....26
Blueprint Guide.....27
Dominion.....28
Nothing or Absolute.....29
One and Many....30

Park Gifts....31
Searching for Real.....32
Who We Are.....33
Mountain Water.....34

Part III: Emails from the Creator

Death.....38
Pen or Paper.....39
Understanding Evil.....40
Sex Games.....41
Hard Times.....42
Prose or Poetry.....43
Master or Slave.....44
Different Views.....45
Why and How....46
Reflections.....47
How and When.....48
Riding the Rock.....49
Pledging Allegiance.....50

Part IV: Father and Child

Searching.....54
Recognizing Love.....55
Karma.....56
War and Peace.....57
Life and Death.....58
Reading the Book.....59
Swinging Pendulum.....60
Ego's Pitfalls.....61

Power of Sound.....62
Tuning In.....64
Open Doors.....65
Concepts of the Mind.....66
Freedom of Spirit.....67
Close As Your Heart.....68
Wisdom and Knowledge.....69
Life's Concerns.....70
Choice and Judgment.....71
Expecting the Unexpected.....72
On the Job.....73
Confronting Fear.....74
Heaven.....75
Color of White.....76
Measuring Distance.....77

Colophon.....79

Snakes Alive

A brief history of snakes and religion

Ancient events have exalted the power of snakes in myth, fable and religion for as long as man has recorded history. Snakes have long been part of Hindu worship; most images of *Lord Shiva* depict snakes around his neck. Puranas have various stories associated with snakes. In the Puranas, *Shesha* is said to hold the world on his many heads and to constantly sing the glories of *Vishnu* from all his mouths.

Snakes also were widely revered in ancient Greece, where the serpent was seen as a healer, and *Asclepius* carried two intertwined on his wand, a symbol seen today on many ambulances. To the Christian, Christ's redemptive work is compared to saving one's life through beholding the *Serpent of brass* (Gospel of John 3:14). The snake is a symbol of the evil one called *Devil, Satan, Beelzebub*. It was a talking snake that tempted Adam and Eve into committing the first sin, thus (as the teaching goes) condemning all who followed to be born as sinners. Snake handling continues in a small number of Christian churches today based on the Bible teachings found in Mark 16:18 and Luke 10:19. Saint Patrick is reputed to have expelled all snakes from Ireland while bringing Christianity to the country in the 5th century, thus explaining the absence of snakes there.

Source: Wikipedia – the free encyclopedia

Fishing for Snakes

Poems herein are designed to stir the snakes hidden in the dark waters of religion and politics. As snakes in the grass bring fear by the poison in their fangs, religious and political snakes flood the mind with poisoned words filled with fear. Fear hides in unexpected places, yet love is as close as a fearless thought. When the snakes of fear are brought to the surface and fully exposed, understanding and wisdom will flood the mind.

Life is like baking apple pies: if you gather the right ingredients to produce the taste you want, carefully mix in measured balance, use the mind as a crust to hold it all together, then bake it in the oven of experience, you get the pie you create, maybe even the one you want. Snake poison or apple pie, there is always a choice.

If I had a wand with a magic beam
that could zap war, I would first
cast it upon the hate, prejudice,
and illusions harbored within
the three religions that sprang
from the bosom of Abraham.
The world might then catch its
breath and get a glimpse of reality.

Part I
Apple Seeds

Apple Seeds I
Original Sin

Naked in evening's cool she walked
the garden, inhaled the fragrance,
consumed its beauty.

The cultivated centerpiece captured
her mind, she circled the magic tree
where hung the forbidden fruit.

A walking-talking snake with words
of allurement appeared; mesmerized
by his fluent forked tongue, she tumbled.

When the serpent said that to eat the sugary
forbidden fruit did not mean death,
but discernment of good and evil,

she bit the apple.

Apple Seeds II
Mystery Woman

With the enigma of the tree
exposed, the apple laid bare,
Eve gave birth to Cain and Abel,

brothers with different dispositions.
Cain a tiller of the soil, Abel
a tender of flocks.

The snake stayed busy
scattering apple seeds among
fields where the brothers worked.

Apples propagated outside the garden
produced hard cider, an intoxicating
drink that cajoled Cain to kill Abel.

After the deed was done, Cain fled
to Nod, took unto himself a wife;
how that woman came to be in Nod

is a secret known only to the snake
and apple seed.

Apple Seeds III
Population Explosion

Adam survived 930 years after
acceding to precepts that populated
the earth; Eve remained in perpetual

pregnancy. Brother to sister, cousin
to cousin contributed to the cause. Cain
and his wife made contributions from over in Nod.

There were giants on the earth in those days
 and the sons of God came and took unto themselves
the daughters of men, giving birth to men of renown.

The giant story angles for answers: was the giant
young David slew with his slingshot
a great-great grandson of a son of God?

The snake and apple seed played games
with pieces of the puzzle.

Apple Seeds IV
Floating the Boat

As mankind multiplied, God saw the snake scattering
apple seeds to seduce human hearts. God repented
the DNA flaw and began research for a righteous man.

When God noticed Noah, He directed him to frame
an ark to house his family plus seven clean and two
unclean of every existing creature that roamed the earth.

Two by two and seven by seven, they marched.
Brachiosaurus was missing from the boarding
list; at 55-100 tons, with its head rising 50 feet

in the air, it would have been a desperate
doorway squeeze for those two giant
reptiles. Forty days and forty nights, rain

came, water rose fifteen cubits above
earth and mountains, every living
substance destroyed, save one olive tree.

Earth full and over flowing, God sent
wind to dry the land, no hint given
as to where all that water blew. It could

be the ice rings that surround Saturn.
The water abated and Noah sent a dove
to determine if it was safe to leave the ark.

On its second trip, the bird bore an olive leaf;
something outside had survived whirling
wind and rain for one hundred fifty days.

The snake and apple seed rode out the storm
on a raft made of fig leaves.

Apple Seeds V
Breeding Division

When next the apple seed took root,
it was in the house of Abraham, two
branches, two different briefings.

One wife, one handmaiden, two sons,
one father: Isaac son of Sarah and Ishmael
issue of Hagar, two treacherous roads traveled.

Isaac fathered Jacob, a.k.a. Israel,
who sired twelve sons, who in
time begot twelve tribes.

Ishmael, banished from the home
of Abraham with his mother Hagar,
wandered in the wilderness of Beersheba.

God promised that Ishmael's twelve sons
would each be prince of a great nation.
Thus, seeds for a family feud were sown.

The snake and apple seed celebrated,
making plans to fuel the fire.

Apple Seeds VI
Bondage for Bread

Joseph loved his coat of many colors given
by father Israel but his brothers were awakened
to anger and subjugated by serpentine words.

The brothers found Joseph in a field, stripped
him of his coat, gave him to Ishmaelite cousins,
who carried him into Egypt to be sold as a slave.

An interpreter of dreams, Joseph found favor
in the eyes of the Pharaoh and became supervisor
over grain storehouses throughout the land.

Famine raged, Joseph's brothers came begging
bread, but the snake had sown seeds in Egyptian minds;
brothers and families were confined in bondage.

The snake sneaked a wink at the apple seed.

Apple Seeds VII
Rods – Snakes – Lice – Frogs

Pharaoh's daughter detected an ark in the river
harboring a boy child. Overcome by compassion,
she took him unto herself and called him Moses.

Moses, the man, murdered an Egyptian, fled
to Median, where he married and kept the flocks
of his father-in-law Jethro. There in a field, God's

words burned from a bush, giving Moses
instructions to rescue the children and lead
them to the land of milk and honey.

After Moses harkened unto the Lord,
he departed for Egypt with wife
and sons. Joined in the wilderness

by brother Aaron, together they went
before the elders to explain God's plan
for saving them from slavery.

When Aaron and Moses approached Pharaoh, the king
rejected their plea, saying, *I do not know your Lord.*
Aaron cast his rod before Pharaoh, and it twisted

and turned into a snake. Pharaoh summoned sorcerers,
who repeated the rod-to-snake trick. The magic show
made headlines for months. Water turned to blood; frogs,

lice and locus infested the land. When the firstborn
of every house lacking blood on the lintel met midnight
massacre, Pharaoh relented. As Moses and the children's

sojourn in the wilderness approached the Red Sea,
Pharaoh repented and sent his army in pursuit,
but the cloud that directed the children by day stood

between the two camps through the night. Morning
dawned, Moses raised his hand, waters parted, children
crossed over, waters closed, Pharaoh's army drowned.

The snake and apple seed slapped hands in celebration.

Apple Seeds VIII
Desert Storm

A cloud by day, pillar of fire by night
led the children; they feasted on manna for
breakfast, quail in the evening.

In constant contact with God, Moses received
Ten Commandments and instructions
on how to buy a servant and sell a daughter.

As rules solidified, an eye for an eye
and a tooth for a tooth became the law
of the land, and woe be unto him that lies

with a beast, for beasts were to be burnt
as an offering and their blood sprinkled
on the altar before the Lord.

Moses made war on all who stood in his way:
he brought death and destruction, taking flocks,
burning villages, and destroying towns.

When his army returned with captives from a battle
with the Midianities, Moses was maddened and ordered
all be killed except virgin woman and girl children:

these, the warriors could keep for themselves.
Moses entered the land of Moab and climbed
Mount Nebo to view the land of Canaan

from afar, for the Lord had forbidden that he
cross over. Thus, having seen the land of his longing,
Moses died at the age of one hundred twenty years.

The snake and apple seed nodded in approval.

Apple Seeds IX
Promised Land

Denoting the death of Moses, the Lord spoke
to Joshua, son of Nun, giving him charge over
the children he once had trusted to Moses.

Joshua told his officers to spread the word
that in three days they would cross over Jordan
to possess land that the Lord had given unto them.

Jericho lay hidden behind a wall. Soon after
crossing the river, Joshua assembled his army
and marched six days around the city. On

the seventh day, trumpets blew, people
shouted, walls tumbled: plundering, burning,
killing and looting was the order of the day.

Joshua directed the devastation until he secured
all that had been promised to Abraham by God.
He then split the spoils among the tribes.

The snake and apple seed
napped beneath an olive tree.

Apple Seeds X
Roman Style

Joshua leased the land among tribes.
According to inheritance, the children
of Judah occupied Jerusalem; but as years

passed, the city was claimed by warring
parties until the day the Roman Legions
came and named Herod as King.

The Lord looked down with frustration:
the flood had failed to cleanse the earth
of the evil Adam and Eve had loosed.

Jesus came teaching love thy neighbor – do good
to them that spitefully use you – when you give
alms don't let your left hand know what

your right hand is doing – the Kingdom of God is
within you, and all these things I do, you can do also;
but when he condemned an eye for an eye, a tooth

for a tooth – said turn the other cheek – criticized
priests who stood on street corners praying in long
flowing robes and turned tables over in the temple –
he was arrested and brought before Pilot to be sentenced
to a Roman-style execution. After death: Jesus appeared
in various places, he had not yet ascended into the ethers.

Some claimed Jesus kept his body but withheld
why he would want worn-out flesh with a pierced
side and nail holes in two hands and both feet.

The snake and apple seed knelt in reverent silence.

Apple Seeds XI
Bible Age

Various versions of the Jesus story traveled
by word of mouth in different direction for decades
before being written into books called Gospels;

therefore, teachings and history of Jesus
were words edited by unknown people.
In time, the new religion reached Rome

and gained proselytes among the Pagans.
Constantine converted church and state
into one governing body.

The Emperor, desiring divisions among
the Bishops concerning church doctrine
be resolved, decreed that a council convene

to write a creed and decide which of the many
books were to be considered Holy Scripture.
Bishops from every region gathered in Nicaea

in 325 AD to negotiate the creed and begin debate
on which books would be sanctified. The contest
continued for a hundred years until a final

Bishops' vote in Rome declared
which books would thereafter be called
The Holy Bible – The Infallible Word of God.

The snake and apple seed roared with laughter

Apple Seeds Exposed
School Days

When the Creator formed the first soul,
He placed it in a garden paradise
to ponder its behavior. Soul, not knowing

who it was or what it was a part of, began
to grumble and groan. The Creator,
realizing Soul would never recognize

its reflection in life's mirror unless it first
learned who it was *not*, created a school
and called it Earth, lessons learned to be
printed on a negative screen. Satan,
a.k.a Snake, earned the post of headmaster.
Each soul entering kindergarten to be issued

coat, energy pack, computer, credit-card –
body, emotion, mind, freewill. Interest
accrued, karma due, at each life cycle's

end. Snake sowed seeds of illusion,
capturing awareness of mind and emotion.
As Soul invalidated one illusion, Snake crafted

a larger one. As in public school, Soul found
grade levels of opportunity to expand awareness
and learn how to love. On graduation day,

Snake hands Soul a diploma. Soul shuts down
its computer, disconnects its power source, sheds
its overcoat, and flies back home to the garden.

The snake and the apple seed hug and snug, yelling,
Well Done!

Part II

Talking

to the

Creator

Talking to the Creator I
Higher Ground

Sitting here on a mountain awaiting
sunrise, I marvel as white fluffy clouds
permeate low valleys and eastern skies blush

myriad reds. New day dawning,
a chance to create fresh choices
and show gratitude for gifts given.

Shall I descend into the valley of clouds
where rotting stumps and slippery rocks
from my yesterdays still dwell,

or shall I take the steep road upward; will
sunset find me holding higher ground
than where this doughty day began?

Talking to the Creator II
Creepy Shadows

When shadows
fill the mind, temples
of man masquerade

as houses of God. When
there is no light, books
written by man claim

birthright to Your
words. When light
pierces darkness,

shadows of books
and temples vanish.
Revealed by the light,

notes written in nature
record reality composed
by Your omnipotent hand.

Talking to the Creator III
Karma – Drama

The flashbacks of past lives
You sent sharpened my vision
of the why-what-how in the *now*.

I thrill at scenes surfacing
through Your karmic law. Though
the stage has changed and costumes

are new, I hail my fellow
actors and their assigned
roles. Reason seen in reruns –

a chance to balance past homage
with increased awareness, opportunities
to be a co-worker in Your timeless plan.

I wear the dress of this drama,
dreaming of cutting-edge costumes
and characters created by actor's choice.

The waters along Your shores
are difficult to navigate, yet simple
when there's knowledge in the oars.

Talking to the Creator IV
Light and Sound

To You who both create and destroy:
when next Your refining light descends
upon my path, please send cirrus clouds
that blindness may not befall me.

As Your bow strokes each unseen
string, let Your voice reverberate
in my heart, but in muted tones
for I am not yet a patron of perfection.

When Your light floods the heavens
and Your celestial symphony plays
throughout the spheres, may the sound
of my voice join in refrain and the spark

in my eye be a candle's flame
upon Your illuminant sea.

Talking to the Creator V
Time Line

The morning news reports You dropped
another poem in northern Arizona
last month, the meteoroid impact

causing a giant crater that sent fragments
over desert sand like words scrolled
across a teleprompter screen.

Like other poems in Your Book, this page
gives us some measure of how long
You've been busy sending messages.

Scientists with poetic eyes and ears who read
this poem tell us it was written three and a half
billion years ago, to us a staggering time;

yet, Your earlier poems indicate neither billions,
trillions, zillions nor can any book written by man
negate the time line posted on Your calendar.

Talking to the Creator VI
Looking for Light

In Your creative design, worlds revolve
around stars, moons around planets,
electrons around their nuclei.

Tiny unseen strings sing the silent
sound of Your music while
meshing life into one mosaic.

Wish that I could sing Your song,
know the words of Your wisdom,
keep body in repair, emotions

under control, utilize energy
efficiently, make my journey into
awareness more effective.

In my causal self may I not
carry past baggage nor
harbor future fears;

rather let me be grounded in now,
using Your gift of reason to treat
life's trials with understanding.

Talking to the Creator VII
Above the Clouds

On my Monday morning walk I
saw strokes of Your brush had tinged
green leaves bright orange and red,
crisp cool air said winter is on the way.

My eyes drew upward beyond
the trees where patches of indigo
blue served as backdrop to gathering
gray clouds. When sunbeams streaked

to tinted foliage, soft winds whispered;

*light is just above the clouds, always
has been, light is eternal.*

Talking to the Creator VIII
Music Within

Eternal Spirit, creator of all
who flies on feathered
wings, swims the deepest

sea, crawls on sandy shores
or burrows beneath earth's clay;
send light to us that walk upright

thinking ourselves superior
to all others; grant that I may
know myself and in turn

learn to know You. In my
seeking, should I find myself
a violin visiting with Your

eternal sound, let my
motif be in sync with Your
celestial music.

If it be my lot to play the flute,
let the brunt of Your breath
compose my song.

Should it be my trust to thump
the drum, let each stroke echo march
time, ever forward, ever upward.

Talking to the Creator IX
Echoes and Reflections

To You whose light
refracted paints the rainbow,

whose echoed voice sings
music of the spheres,

grant that I be polished in Your
prism, reflected in Your painted print.

Let my voice be echoed in Your music,
middle C in tune with silent song,

that in this earthly journey I now
travel, I learn to choose the right

and know the wrong.

Talking to the Creator X
Blueprint Guide

Patterns in Your designs
make magic in the round.
Moon is round, earth
is round, sun is round.

Moon circles earth
earth circles sun,
galaxies go
'round and 'round.

Atoms are round,
electrons in
flawless motion
go 'round and 'round.

Winter chases spring,
summer chases fall,
year after year
'round and 'round.

Applying Your blueprint,
is there reason I should
think life and death
to be of different design?

Talking to the Creator XI
Dominion

Can humankind's politics,
myths, fables, legends, wars
or religious dogma come
to comprehend

a billion galaxies
with a billion stars,
rotating planets with life

fresh from trees,
beings light years ahead
of our imagination? Please

say You did not give
earthly man dominion
over all!!

Talking to the Creator XII
Nothing or Absolute

Views of whom or what You are
and questions of whether You even exist
cascade unabated in human minds.

Many have created You in *their* image
and see You sitting on a throne of judgment
dispensing rewards and punishments

for good and evil; others see You as nothing,
a non-existent figure of religious imagination
instituted by diluted minds.

Electrons circle their nuclei, billions
of planets circle millions of stars,
what unseen force wrote these laws?

Who gave the flower its fragrance?
If it be a gift from the God of Judgment,
for what was the flower being rewarded?

If the flower's scent springs from a void,
in what magic vial was the sweet smell
mixed, and how did nothing shape the stars?

Could it be You are No-Thing, yet essence
of All-Things, a song in every heart, waiting
to be sung?

Talking to the Creator XIII
One and Many

In early spring
I watched two robins
swirl in the air,
dance on the ground,
mate and build a nest.

In early summer
four babies fledged,
abandoned the nest,
learned to fly
and search for food.

In early fall,
male, female
and offspring
gathered together
and flew south.

Now I understand
what You have been
trying to tell me,

when two become one,
the one becomes many.

Talking to the Creator XIV
Park Gifts

As I walk in the park today, sweet
scent of honeysuckle rides the wind,
warm sunrays light my path.

Morning mist on my face brings fresh
visions to mind of prolific days;
hints of progress foreshadow new purpose.

High in an old oak tree, a mocking
bird sings a song of joy; he sings
for the sparrow, sings for the lark.

In the moment's beauty,
the ambiance of light and sound
are symphony to eyes and ears.

Clearly these gifts are not for me alone
but for all who walk this way longing
to listen to words written in Your book.

Talking to the Creator XV
Searching for Real

Creator of all that lives, where can I find You?
Have I probed and probed the recess of my
mind and depth of imagination, in vain?

Can I, by affirmation or ritual, persuade You
to reveal Yourself, shall I listen for Your voice
in words of orators orchestrating in government

halls, will I find Your truth echoing from portals
of pulpits, cathedrals, temples and holy shrines?
Have You meandered to the mosque,

can I meet You at the Wailing Wall, are You
hiding in the judge's chamber? Are You the inner voice
speaking in my quiet contemplation? Did I hear You

say life, like the four seasons, springs forth, matures,
retreats, springs forth again? Is it You whispering
in the wind, saying the coming darkness

is only a backdrop on which to paint the new dawn?
I review Your radiant beauty from the shadows
of my mind, wish that I could stand in Your pure light.

I witness Your solemn stillness on which
my every move is etched; I hear the silence
of Your sound that echoes my every word.

Although my mind cannot fathom the complete
depth of Your countenance, I see You through
windows of my heart, and in silent-stillness

You stand naked: stripped of Your mask.

Talking to the Creator XVI
Who We Are

I see in truth we are souls –
droplets of awareness

in Your ocean of wisdom

progenies of Your creation

flickering candles on a sea of light

actors on stage

receptors of faculty

practitioners of life

witnesses to death

neophytes –
in Your workshop of love

Talking to the Creator XVII
Mountain Water

Sitting by a mountain stream
my mind follows rushing
water as it flows over rocks
and down a mountain to rivers
that flow into rivers that flow
into rivers on their way to the sea.

From ocean waters a mist will rise
to drifting clouds and ride swift
winds back to layered hills where
droplets drain into deepening brooks
and once again join rushing water
running over rocks and down

the mountain to join a river
that joins a river to meander its way
to salty seas. Here in silent peace
of rugged mountains, with sounds
of water replenishing repose,
I realize why You design

in cycles. The singing water
of mountain streams, soon
to return in morning
mist, reminds me that I
too am a mountain stream
rushing to a mystical sea.

Part III

Emails

from the Creator

Email from the Creator I
Death

I see questions:

You want to know if death
can hit a delete button
and cancel life.

If your car wears out
you send it to the junkyard,
then purchase another. Death

can cancel the physical,
emotional and mental bodies
but has no power over soul,

the designated driver.

Email from the Creator II
Paper or Pen

I see you are troubled
over darkness and light, pain
and suffering; why do I allow it?

Have you ever tried writing
with black pen on black paper
or white on white?

If you are to know Me, you must
understand what I am not,
lest you be lost in illusion.

I give you black on white,
white on black, so you can learn
which is paper and which is pen.

Email from the Creator III
Understanding Evil

I see you are confused over
the evil one, the one you call
Devil, Satan, Beelzebub.

He is the master of education,
his chalk is deceit,
his blackboard illusion.

You might be surprised to know
he works for me. He is the mirror
that reflects fears and perverse passions

in your mind. He comes disguised in many
robes, you know him best when he adorns
his horns and slithers like a snake, yet

his finest ruse is when he retreats
behind sanctified walls and speaks
from his pedestal of sanctity.

As the spider weaves its web to trap
the fly, so does he weave his words
to malign the mental flow.

From his illusions, you must break free
if ever you are to know my world.
Keep foremost in your mind

that wherever you are,
you have arrived on the wings
of your own thoughts.

Email from the Creator IV
Sex Games

I see questions of male
and female are meandering
through your mind.

Which should dominate,
how do they relate
to each other, is woman

just a helpmate for man?
Both male and female principles
reside within you, two working

parts of the same whole.
Some lives you are male,
other times you are female,

a necessary step in the
course of your enlightenment.
When you have entwined

these two entities within,
when male is female,
and female is male,

when love has melted two
into one, you will be able to say,

In my soul, I am free.

Email from the Creator V
Hard Times

I see you are in a dilemma
over disasters. Let Me
remind you of My law
of cause and effect, reaping
what you sow.

Greed, in search of fossil
fuel, ignores the renewable
resources I provide,
causing the globe to warm
and oceans to rise.

The warmer the water,
the stronger the storm.
Fighting war under false
pretense reduces resources
that could be employed to save

those enveloped in a sea
of sorrow. The devil pays the devil
his due, while I wait patiently
to welcome those who learned
to love their neighbors.

Email from the Creator VI
Prose or Poetry

I see you begin
to understand. My words
are written throughout creation,
not in books written by man.

This is good; I have much to teach
in earthly classrooms. As myth
and legends are exposed,
awareness expands.

Each learning cycle brings
new levels of adventure; life
ebbs and flows like ocean
waves meeting the shore.

Some waves gently caress the sand,
others churn the deepest depths, wash
waste to the surface and ferry
decay out to sea.

When your awareness goes beyond
illusions, you will marvel at the beauty
of reality. Truth is wind beneath
the wings of soul.

Email from the Creator VII
Master or Slave

You are confused over karma,
cause and effect, reaping what you sow.
You complain when you perceive
injustice, some seeming to receive

more than they deserve while others
experience great suffering. A restrictive
perspective leads to confusing conclusions.
If you are to understand the process

you must expand your thoughts,
go beyond emotion before you
make judgments. He who once
was master may now be slave, while

he who was slave, could now be
master. Do not be troubled
that some seem favored over others:
the seeds sown in today's season

may not sprout until a distant spring.
It matters not master or slave, black
or white, male or female; it is all
two parts of the same whole. When

you learn to balance the coin
of life on its edge, neither side will
outweigh the other, and you can
roll along with a sense of purpose.

Email from the Creator VIII
Different Views

You wrestle with the words
of your attackers because
their faith is not your troth.

Be not disturbed, you must
understand they, too, are students
in My school. In time

all will graduate to a higher state.
For now, you must visit opposite
views on your way to enlightenment.

They who scorn are part of your
education, hidden in their score lies
opportunity to learn right from wrong.

Email From the Creator IX
Why and How

There are some whys
bouncing around in your head:

why you face stressful situations,
why obstacles are present on your path,
why certain people come into your life.

In My classrooms, stress and obstacles
are the pencils and paper I provide
so you can write your story on life's scroll.

People you meet are mirrors
reflecting contentious forces
that linger from your past.

To turn reflections to positive
pictures, surf on the surface,
examine every color in white light.

Be not detracted by deflections,
rather let disruptions be a guide
to staying centered and in balance;

enlightenment fully engages
on the middle path.

Email from the Creator X
Reflections

I am the sun
you are moon,
only in reflection
will you see Me.

Cloaked in darkness,
My light surrounds you,
yet yours is the gift
of a million mirrors.

My words are engraved
throughout creation;
if you reflect the light,
you can read My book.

Email from the Creator XI
How and When

I see you are considering how
creation began, how will it end,
what it's purpose could be.

The simple answer is, it has no
beginning, no end. The creative
process just is, always has been.

Time is a tedious note on the path
of understanding in the human
mind. Contemplate

how life moves in cycles,
the smallest unit within
the atom sings a silent song.

When you hear the music,
waltz with the movement;
harmony is key to seeing,

discords are fear, ego and greed;
the results are recorded in karma's
annals of cause and effect.

Email from the Creator XII
Riding the Rock

Thoughts circle in your mind
concerning patterns in My creation.
You ride a round rock through space

around a gaseous ball of fire that drags
a solar system around the center
of a galaxy with a billion stars.

Mimicking life and death, protons
transform into neutrons, while neutrons
become protons through beta decay.

I use this pattern to give you opportunity
to make adjustment, correct mistakes
and come to know Me, one step at a time.

As spring bursts forth, slides into summer,
gives way to fall, retreats to winter to spring
forth again, so does the life you now live.

Given this as the method I have chosen to manage
my universal school, why would I change My
pattern when it comes to life and death?

Emails from the Creator XIII
Pledging Allegiance

Religious confusion with conflict
whirls through your mind; believers
from left and right battle for your

allegiance to their cause. Left versus
right, two sides of the same coin; truth
is found on the middle path. Believers

hold fast to faith, believing their
religious teachings are absolute
and must be spread to all.

Non-believers are believers in *disguise,*
placing faith in *nothing,* holding the belief
that phenomena just happen.

Endless flip-flops, side-to-side, heads
up, tails down, heads down,
tails up, a battle laced with ego

in fear of losing power over people.
If you would be a true seeker of truth,
you must bring your thoughts into balance.

Turn the coin on its edge, and you can roll
on down the road to discovery.

Part IV

Father and Child

Father and Child I
Searching

Father, my father,
reveal life's meaning
to my mind, make
known to me the path
of enlightenment.

My child, my child,
let self awareness be
your utopia. You are soul,
a raindrop in the Creator's
ocean of wisdom and love.

Let no earthly desire
deter you from expanding
awareness lest
in the distilling you
reap an empty cup.

Rather, hold your dreams
as near to your heart as
you would your newborn
child. What you cultivate today
will be your cache tomorrow.

Father and Child II
Recognizing Love

Father, my father,
show me the way
to the summit of love.

My child, my child, I have
no words to will you
there, love is not a destination
but a terrace traveled.

Love is the light
in wisdom's eye,
a way of life longing
to be explored.

Search not for love
in some perfected paradise;
love is a shadow stalking
your every step,

hoping for adoption.

Father and Child III
Karma

Father, my father,
is there no justice
in this wicked world?

My child, my child,
every deed has its avenue
of return to its place of birth.

As the boomerang whirls
away and back again, so does
each word flung from your tongue
fly unseen around your future.

Should the circle of time
be in minutes or millennia,
it is constantly in motion.
Karma never forgets.

At unexpected moments
old actions reappear
begging for balance
and resolution,

and you will say
I don't deserve this,

is there no justice?

Father and Child IV
War and Peace

Father, my father,
why do people fight wars?

My child, my child,
mankind passes preconceptions
from generation to generation
through politics and religion.

Believers search not for truth
but confirmation of established
beliefs, each religion touting
their creed worthy of life and death.

Truth is like direct sunlight, much
too powerful for the human eye, yet
when refracted it can be reviewed
as separate rays.

Political and religious believers cling
to their most cherished beam, regarding
all others as enemies, never realizing truth's
light converts the rainbow spectrum into one.

In your search for wisdom, adjust
your eyes to every color, that you
may witness the full arc embodied
in the white light of love.

Father and Child V
Life and Death

Father, my father,
why do people die?

My child, my child, have no fear
of death, the body is but an agent
of expression for soul's awareness.

Soul begins its incarnated journey in naive
innocence, cantering the circled path
that teaches the Creator's way.

The highway to enlightenment is long
and hard. To know what love is, soul
must learn what love is not.

Central to this concept are the positive
and negative forces that do battle within
to misguide mind and mislead emotions.

Just as you may acquire several automobiles
to proceed in this present life, soul will bear
many bodies in its longing for love.

Be attentive at every station, ask questions
at every stop; beware of distorted words designed
to mangle the mind and alter awareness.

Life is not yesterday's mistakes
nor tomorrow's dreams; life is soul
on a journey, every nano is now.

Father and Child VI
Reading the Book

Father, my father, is there
a book I can trust to lead me
to enlightenment?

My child, my child, there
is such a book, but not
on the library shelf.

Not only may you read this book,
you may be a contributing character
within its pages.

When you see sunrise in the east
and sunset in the west, you are reading
the Creator's law of circled motion.

That which goes around will return,
giving opportunity to write, edit
and rewrite every day of your life.

So is it written in the unseen
world of atoms, quarks and strings
as they sing creation's story.

Let your voice be a joyous song
in harmony with the Creator's
symphony of light and sound.

In nature's world you can witness
the written laws of life, the only book
ever composed by the Creator's hand.

Father and Child VII
Swinging Pendulum

Father, my father,
joy and sorrow swing
like a pendulum within me.
How can I make it stop?

My child, my child,
your thoughts and emotions
run in cycles like the rising
and setting of the sun.

Artists paint and poets write
to capture the beauty of
sunrise and sunset, yet
they are illusions.

Should you travel into outer space,
you would see that the sun never rises,
nor does it set; it is a continuous
fire in the heavens.

If you cut the chains of ego, soul can rise
into the radiant ethers, where you see joy
and sorrow, like the sun, entwine into one
complete learning experience.

Father and Child VIII
Ego's Pitfall

Father, my father,
how can I make my mark
so that the world will
acknowledge who I am?

My child, my child,
you must sever the cord
of self-seeking; extended
in time, ego burns to ashes.

Let your life be of service
to others. On that road, you
will meet open minds
with answers to questions

and true purpose will burst
into bloom. As you make
your way along highways

and byways, reserve in your
heart a reverence for all life.
The same power that created
valleys with mountain views,
created you.

Father and Child IX
Power of Sound

Father, my father,
why do people chant and pray?

My child, my child,
some people in their prayers
seek to fulfill desires,

others pray in desperation,
while many give thanks
for gifts received.

Those tracing inner truth chant
their mantra to quiet the mind
and open doors to soul

and new inspiration.
Heard or unheard
sound is triumphant,

throughout creation.
Atemporal atoms and quarks
are minutely in motion;

tiny little strings vibrating
according to orientation
sing the silent song of life.

The sound of prayers and chants are
drawn to the vibes they mimic as
radio waves are attracted to a tuner.

So my child, choose words
with care lest they be a pitfall
to understanding.

The words you speak
today will be your
song tomorrow.

Father and Child X
Tuning In

Father, my father,
must I see it, to believe it?.

My child, my child,
the eye and ear detect
echoes and reflections.

Like television signals
moving unseen
in search of a receiver,

life's deeper reality
glides through the ethers,
longing for soul's recognition.

If your desire is truth, set
your dial on awareness,
open your heart to love,

your mind to life's new song.

Father and Child XI
Open Doors

Father, my Father,
teach me the prayer I should pray,
that I might live a successful life.

My child, my child, you must not
ask the Creator to do for you what can
only be done through you.

As electricity flows from
a power house to light homes
and bring scenes to screens,

the creative power predominates
inner space in search of avenues
for multiple manifestation.

If you desire a dynamic life, open the doors
of your heart and mind to a marriage of worlds
within, and the creative power will find you.

Father and Child XII
Concepts of the Mind

Father, my father,
speak to me the words
that will lead to truth.

My child, my child,
I cannot give you truth
but only concepts of my mind

that you may or may not
believe. Truth is found
on the path of experience.

If you are to see life
from a lofty viewpoint,
perception must rise beyond

the pendulum of emotion
and monkeys of the mind.
Let each experience

be measured into your mind
and weighed on the balance
beam of reason.

When experience and reason
are in refined execution,
consciousness will expand

and the precepts of soul
will prepare new visions
to form clear perimeters.

Father and Child XIII
Freedom of Spirit

Father, my father, so many
religions claim title to truth,
which one should I serve?

My child, my child,
be neither slave nor master
in your search for enlightenment,

for the master is held in servitude
by the needs of his followers, and slaves
are manipulated by their master's words.

If you would find your true self
and be free of attachments, you must
give equal weight to that which is left

and that which is right. When you have balanced
the yin and yang in your mind, you will be free
to follow the middle path to higher awareness.

Father and Child XIV
Close as Your Heart

Father, my father,
how far is it to heaven?

My child, my child,
the highway to heaven
is not measured in miles.

The cobblestone lane is laden
with clever steps that will lead
to knowledge of your true self

upon arrival. Heaven is closer
than your heartbeat, yet distant

as your degree of understanding.
The road to heaven is measured
by markers of realization. Facts

are tools, enlightenment the milepost:
each moment an opportunity to move
forward, one step at a time.

Father and Child XV
Wisdom and Knowledge

Father, my father,
what is the key
to enlightenment?

My child, my child,
the keys to enlightenment
are wisdom and charity;

they unlock the door
that leads to freedom.
Do not confuse facts

with wisdom, for knowledge
is an instrument created by man
to be used as a search engine.

Wisdom is perception of soul,
procured through life's experiences
and exposed through tools of knowledge.

Do not be deceived by believing
charity flows only downward
from the Creator. If ever

you are to find enlightenment, love
must return to its source through
you. So grasp the keys of wisdom

and charity firmly in the hands
of knowledge, and study the path
that leads to freedom.

Father and Child XVI
Life's Concerns

Father, my father,
what should my concern be
in my search for self?

My child, my child, the power
of emotion is like a magnet

to iron. Beware the gravity
of passions that cling like
glue in caverns of the mind.

Lust,
an excessive appetite
for pleasure of the senses,
consumes innovation.

Anger,
emotion on fire,
strikes a deadly flame
to all within its path.

Greed,
a cousin to lust, son
of ego, traps unsuspecting
prey in its claws.

Vanity,
an aggrandized vision of self,
cares for none other.

Attachment
traps soul in a cage
and clips its wings.

My child, beware mind's passions;
when tossed together like a salad,
they digest in the dark of night.

Father and Child XVII
Choice and Judgment

Father, my father,
when is judgment day?

My child, my child,
today we post, tomorrow
we read and rewrite.

Judgment day is today,
for every choice you make
awaits your tomorrow.

Let each thought be a child
of experience and every
action be born of thought.

Choose each step with care;
today you choose,
tomorrow you judge.

Father and Child XVIII
Expecting the Unexpected

Father, my father,
how can I avoid having my plans
unhinged by the unexpected?

My child, my child, if you
retreat from surprise, you are
losing serious lessons of life.

When you go to school,
is it not something new
and startling you learn?

Do not let fear keep you from
your chosen goals; rather, make
space in your plans

for the unpredictable. When
you integrate your plans,
it gives you unexpected

control over the unexpected.

Father and Child XIX
On the Job

Father, my father,
how shall I choose
my life's work?

My child, my child,
work is the tuning fork of soul;
it can bring guidance and purpose
or grief and despair to your life.

It matters not the choice,
but that you find purpose;
resolve equals happiness,
and joy is its own reward.

Let work today be your best
and tomorrow an improvement
through lessons learned.

Welcome each morning
with expectation of success
and apply each precept

to your every moment.

Father and Child XX
Confronting Fear

Father, my father,
how can I overcome
my fear of life's failures?

My child, my child,
it is not the failures but fear
itself that haunts your mind.

The roar of thunder before
the storm gives opportunity
to face your fears. When

the rain is gone, the rainbow
will appear in the sky.
Your teeth go unnoticed

until the toothache;
then you face the fear
of the dental drill.

Life's thunder is like
a toothache. Don't let your
fears stand in the way

of your trip to the dentist.

Father and Child XXI
Heaven

Father, my father,
will heaven ever
come to earth?

My child, my child,
if this world was perfect,
there would be one too many

heavens and no way for soul
to learn how to live and love.
To give soul the chance

to grow and become aware,
the Creator created this school
based on positive and negative

forces. Here soul receives
lessons in how to love.
My child, that is why heaven

will never come to earth.

Father and Child XXII
Color of White

Father, my father,
how can I know good from evil?

My child, my child,
good and evil are like
rainbows: when mingled,
they can be black or white.

White light, the source of all
color, in absence renders
black. Red, blue, green
primaries paired,

turn to cyan, magenta
yellow; mixed in triplet return
to white. Subtractive colors
in duo produce white,

in trio vanish to black.
My child, if you would
understand good and evil,
study patterns of color,

scrutinize those who distort
rainbow rays for gain. In their
conjoined message, black
often masquerades as white.

Father and Child XXIII
Measuring Distance

Father, my father,
how far to heaven,
how fast can I get there?

My child, my child,
heaven and hell are as close
as your state of awareness,

yet it may take many lifetimes
to survey the distance. Avoid
mind's winding roads,

keep positive and negative
forces in balance. The middle path
is the short way home.

How fast you travel depends
on your choices put into action.
Perfect speed is being there.

Colophon

Text and Titles
set in Chaparral Pro
with Adobe Indesign
printed in USA

onespiritpress@gmail.com
www.onespiritpress.com

www.ingramcontent.com/pod-product-compliance
Lightning Source LLC
Chambersburg PA
CBHW070654050426
42451CB00008B/346